A ROOKIE READER

RAIN! RAIN!

By Carol Greene

Illustrations by Larry Frederick

Prepared under the direction of Robert Hillerich, Ph.D.

CHILDRENS PRESS ™

CHICAGO

This book is for Becky.

Library of Congress Cataloging in Publication Data

Greene, Carol.
  Rain! Rain!

  (A Rookie reader)
  Summary: Black clouds bring lightning and
thunder and finally, rain that falls on every-
thing and everyone. Includes a word list.
  [1. Rain and rainfall—Fiction]
I. Frederick, Larry, ill.   II. Title.
III. Series.
PZ7.G82845Rai 1982   [E]   82-9509
ISBN 0-516-02034-X   AACR2

Rain? Rain?

Will it?

Will it rain?

One cloud.

Two clouds.

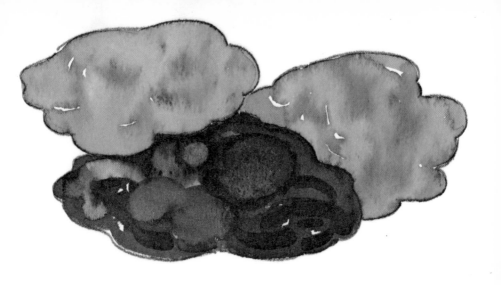

Black clouds.

Blue clouds.

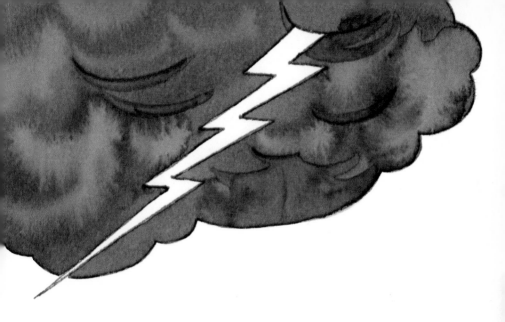

Lightning pop.

Thunder drum.

Rain! Rain!

See it come.

Rain on trees.

Rain on bees.

Rain on trucks.

Rain on ducks.

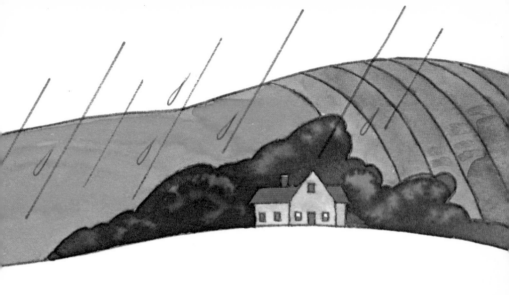

Rain on towns.

Rain on clowns.

Rain on roof.

Plop. Plop.

Rain on window.

Drop. Drop.

Rain on me.

Rain on you.

Come, see!

Rain in…

PUDDLES!

WORD LIST

bees
black
blue
cloud
clouds
clowns
come
drop
drum

ducks
in
it
lightning
me
on
one
plop
pop
puddles

rain
roof
see
thunder
towns
trees
trucks
two
will
window
you

About the Author

Carol Greene has written over 20 books for children, plus stories, poems, songs, and filmstrips. She has also worked as a children's editor and a teacher of writing for children. She received a B.A. in English Literature from Park College, Parkville, Missouri, and an M.A. in Musicology from Indiana University. Ms. Greene lives in St. Louis, Missouri. When she isn't writing, she likes to read, travel, sing, do volunteer work at her church — and write some more. Her *The Super Snoops and the Missing Sleepers* and *Sandra Day O'Connor, First Woman on the Supreme Court* have also been published by Childrens Press.

About the Artist

Larry Frederick is a native of Chicago who now works as a free-lance illustrator in Evanston, Illinois. He studied at the art center school in Los Angeles, California as well as several art schools in the Chicago area. He began his career in advertising art, but for the past fourteen years has worked mainly in book illustration.